Jesus Raises a Little Girl to Life

A Miracle in Capernaum

Jim Reimann

Illustrations by Rony Tamir

In Capernaum lived Jairus, whose little girl was near death,
So he asked Jesus to touch her, so she would live and have breath.
Jairus ruled the synagogue where other miracles were done,
Thus he had faith in Jesus—God's healing, miraculous One.

Yet several men came to Jairus, while he still pleaded and cried,
Saying, “Don’t bother this man anymore; your daughter has died.”
But Jesus told poor Jairus, “Do not be afraid; just believe;
Your daughter will live, there’s no need for you and your wife to grieve.”

As they came to the man's house, Jesus saw a large, noisy crowd,
"Go away. The girl is not dead, but asleep," He said aloud.
But the people laughed and mocked Him—it was quite a commotion,
They showed the Lord no proper respect, or any devotion.

Jesus walked into the house, with only Peter, John, and James,
He was about to confirm who He was, proving all His claims.
Taking the dead girl by the hand, and with love in His eyes,
Jesus said, “Talitha koum!”—meaning, “Little girl, arise!”

The girl's spirit returned, and she immediately stood,
Proving the Word of the great Physician, a Savior so good.
All the people were now quite amazed and very astonished,
"But don't tell anyone about this," Christ Jesus admonished.

Yet in spite of what Jesus said, the news of His healing hand
Spread across the region of Galilee and throughout the land.
So, dear boys and girls, when you need the Lord's healing touch,
Go to Him in prayer, for He loves His children so very much.

www.JimReimann.com

Rev. Jim Reimann
Israel Tour Leader of 25+ Pilgrimages
Editor of the Updated Editions of:
My Utmost for His Highest (Oswald Chambers)
Streams in the Desert (Lettie Cowman)
Morning by Morning (Charles Spurgeon)
Evening by Evening (Charles Spurgeon)

ISBN: 978-965-7607-23-7

Printed by GESTELIT
info@gestelit.co.il

Printed in the Holy Land

For ordering information, please contact the publisher:
Intelecty, Ltd.
76 Hagalil
Nofit, Israel 36001
Tel: 97249930922
Fax: 972722830147
Mobile: 972523348598
galit@gestelit.co.il
jesusbooks4kids.com

Also in this series:

Jesus is Born! The Bethlehem Story
Jesus is Alive! The Empty Tomb in Jerusalem
John 3:16 Jesus and Nicodemus in Jerusalem
Jesus Loves the Little Children of the World
Saul is Born Again The Conversion of the Apostle Paul
Stephen - The First Christian Martyr A Story from Jerusalem
Jesus Heals a Little Boy A Miracle in Capernaum
The Baptism of Jesus A Story from the Jordan River
The Jesus Boat

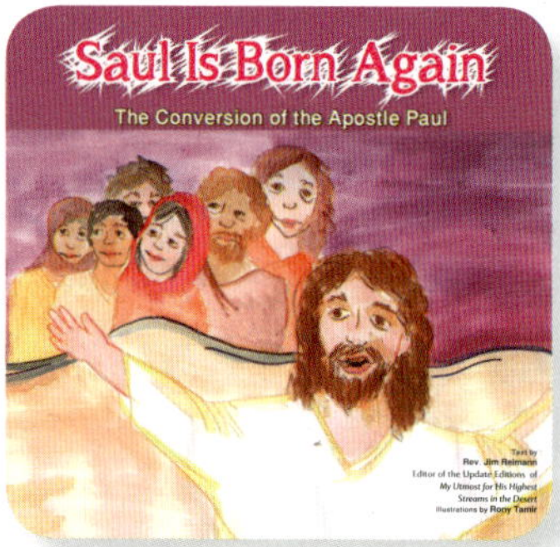
Saul Is Born Again
The Conversion of the Apostle Paul

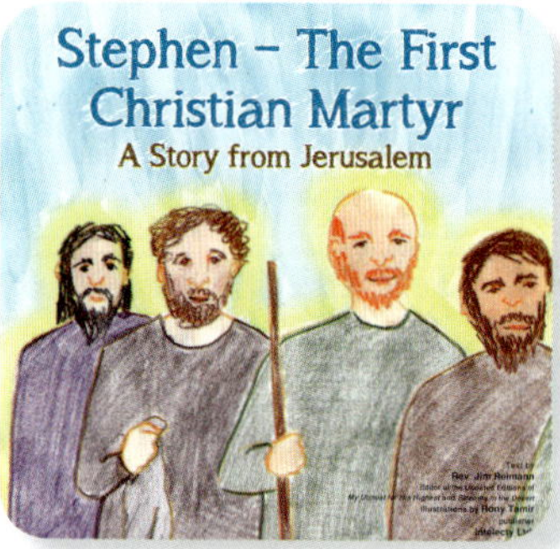
Stephen – The First Christian Martyr
A Story from Jerusalem

The Jesus Boat

John 3:16
Jesus and Nicodemus in Jerusalem
Text by Rev Jim Reimann
Editor of the Updated Editions of
My Utmost for His Highest and Streams in the Desert
Illustrations by Julia Filipone Erez

NO POTATO
NO TOMATO
Life in the Time of Jesus

The Baptism of Jesus
A Story from the Jordan River

The Ballad of MAGDALA

Caesarea–
A Glimpse at the Past of a Glorious City
English Version: Joseph S. Bloch
Illustrations: Nataliya Chernysheva

Jesus Heals a Little Boy
A Miracle in Capernaum

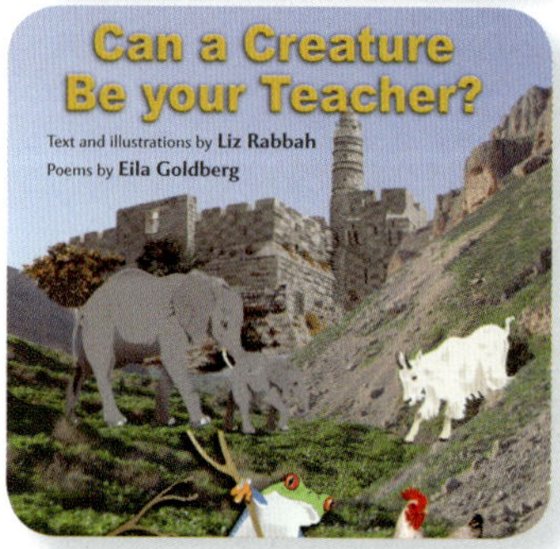
Can a Creature Be your Teacher?
Text and illustrations by Liz Rabbah
Poems by Eila Goldberg